KUMBH MELA

ISBN : 81-88043-66-4

First Edition 2010

Winsome Books India

E-mail : winsomebooks@rediffmail.com
admin@winsomebooks.com
Website : www.winsomebooks.com

KUMBH MELA

By Deepak Kumar Singh

Winsome Books India

Maha Kumbh Mela at Prayag

One of the major Hindu religious occasions, the Kumbh Mela occurs four times every twelve years and rotates among four hallowed locations: Allahabad (Prayag), Haridwar, Ujjain and Nashik where the sacred drops of the mythical amrita (nectar) from the Amrtit Kumbh (urn of nectar) are said to have fallen. Once every twelve years the planets align in a configuration eagerly awaited by millions of devotees. It is time for Haridwar Kumbha Mela. The Kumbh Mela at Haridwar takes place when the planet Jupiter enters Aquarius and the Sun enters Aries. The observance of Kumbh Mela witnesses a mass Hindu pilgrimage and a great confluence of thousands of holy men and women. The event is also attended by thousands of tourists from the world over. It is stated to be the largest mass gathering on the earth.

GAYATRI MATRA

AUM BHOOR BHUWAH SWAHA,
TAT SAVITUR VARENYAM
BHARGO DEVASAYA DHEEMAHI
DHIYO YO NAHA PRACHODAYAT.

ऊँ भूर्भुवः स्वः
तत्सवितुर्वरेनयं
भर्गो देवस्य धीमहि
धीयो यो नः प्रचोदयात्।।

Oh God! Thou art the Giver of Life,
Remover of pain and sorrow,
The Bestower of happiness,
Oh! Creator of the Universe,
May we receive thy supreme sin-destroying light,
May Thou guide our intellect in the right direction.

LEGENDS OF KUMBH MELA

The legendry churning of ocean

Naga sadhus proceeding to the banks of Ganges at Prayag

The origin of the Kumbh Mela goes down to mythology. One of the earliest references to it is in the Atharva Veda, which says that Brahma (the Creator of the Universe) set up the tradition to liberate and purify the human soul. Some experts date the origin of the Kumbh Mela to Neolithic times.

There are myths galore regarding the origin of Kumbh Mela. All of them can be traced back to the Puranas. The most important and widely accepted myth starts in the Bhagavatha Purana.

Puranas are filled with wars between Devas (demi-gods) and Asuras (demons). The Devas always have the upper hand but occasionally due to some curse or misdeeds the Devas lose this upper hand.

Lord Indra, the king of Devas, was once cursed by Sage Durvasa and as the result of this curse, Demons overpowered the Devas. To find a solution the Devas approached Lord Vishnu. Lord Vishnu advised them to obtain Amrit - 'the nectar of immortality.'

To obtain the Amrit the Devas should churn the ocean. Mandara Mountain agreed to be the churning rod and Vasuki, the serpent agreed, to be the rope. To churn the ocean the Devas needed the help of Asuras as the Devas could only hold one-end of the rope. But Devas was not willing to share the Amrit with Asuras. Finally, without any other choice the Devas agreed to share the Amrit with the Asuras.

Churning started and the ocean started to yield divine gifts. Amrit was the last to appear. Dhanvantari, the physician of the gods, appeared with Amrit. The Asuras took the Amrit and started to run away. A fight between the Devas and Asuras ensued.

All the myths associated with Kumbh Mela are the same till this point. But the story changes from this point in different myths.

In Skanda Purana, it is suggested that Indra's son Jayanta got hold of the Amrit during the fight between the Devas and Asuras. He started to run away with it. The demons started to chase Jayanta around the earth. The chase lasted for 12 days or 12 human years, One day of Devas is equal to one human year, During this time, the nectar spilled at Allahabad, Haridwar, Nasik and Ujjain.

Another legend of Kumbha Mela appears in Vishnu Purana, Brahmananda Purana, Padma, Agni Purana, the Mahabharata and the Ramayana. It suggests that as soon as Dhanvantari appeared with Amrit, Lord Vishnu passed it to Garuda, the mythical bird and vehicle of Lord Vishnu. Asuras chased Garuda for 12 days or 12 human years. And Garuda stopped and the nectar spilled at Allahabad, Haridwar, Nasik and Ujjain.

Naga sadhu chanting hymns in praise of the Ganges

HISTORY OF KUMBH MELA

Chinese traveler Hiuen Tsang

The exact origin of the Kumbh Mela is very hard to pinpoint. The fair is a primitive one and the reason it is held can be traced back to the ancient episode of 'Sagar Manthan' or 'Churning of the Ocean'.

It is not exactly known since when did people begin to hold Kumbh Mela at the four places of its celebration. It is widely known how this spectacle of faith has attracted the curiosity of foreign travellers from time to time. The famous seventh century Chinese traveller Hiuen-Tsang was probably the first person to mention Kumbh Mela in his diary. Hiuen-Tsang gave an eyewitness account of Kumbh Mela reporting how during the Hindu month of Magha (January-February) half a million people had assembled on the banks of the river Ganges at Allahabad to observe a celebration for 75 days.

He also wrote that the pilgrims to the fair assembled along with their king, his ministers, scholars, philosophers and sages. The king had donated huge amounts of gold, silver, and jewels in charity to acquire good merit and assure his place in heaven. This indicates that Kumbh Mela was already quite popular in the seventh century.

In the eight century, the great Indian saint Shankara popularized the Kumbh Mela among the common people. As a natural consequence, with each passing year the fair began to be attended by more and more people. The holy ritual of taking a bath in the holy river waters is a must for all devotees.

The sacred Hindu scriptures stress on having the guidance of a spiritual leader who has acquired the knowledge of the self. Only such a realized person can impart one the true knowledge and show him/her the path towards spiritual fulfillment. The great Shankara placed special importance to the opportunity of associating with saintly persons while at Kumbh Mela. Hence, both hearing from sadhus (holy men) and sacred bathing are still the two main purposes of the pilgrims thronging Kumbh Mela.

By 1977, the number of pilgrims attending Kumbh Mela had grown to a record 15 million.! By 1989, the attendance was approximately 29 million - nearly double that of the previous record. Today, around 60 million people is said to attend the Maha Kumbh Mela, making it the largest gathering anywhere in the world.

Every year the Indian government spends a large sum on preliminary organisation for the Kumbh Mela. Adequate arrangements are made to provide for pure drinking water, food, transportation, electrical facilities; sanitation; security measures and medical assistance. Despite such arrangements, casualties of human lives occur frequently. But this hardly deters the spirit of the pilgrims to the fair whose number goes on increasing with each passing year.

Words can hardly describe the phenomenon that the Kumbh Mela is. It is one event that has to be experienced personally.

Adi Shankar

PLACES OF KUMBH MELA

Every year, periodical or annual fairs are held on river banks, lake-shores, beaches and sacred places by pious Hindus to commemorate important events mentioned in their sacred scriptures or in honour of their Gods or Goddesses. This is observed in almost every state of India.

The observance of Kumbh Mela is believed to have started thousands of years ago, in the Vedic period. The ancient Vedic text of Bhagavat Purana describes how in the early days of creation demi-gods and demons made a temporary agreement to churn the Ksheera Sagara (primordial ocean of milk) together for the amrit (the nectar of immortality) and to share the nectar equally. However, on the sight of the Amrita-Kumbh (urn of nectar), the two sides engaged themselves in a fierce battle for its possession. In this battle that continued for twelve days and twelve nights (equivalent to twelve human years), drops of the sacred amrita is believed to have spilled over to four place on earth - Prayag, Haridwar, Ujjain and Nasik.

Therefore, these four locations are considered holy by the Hindus and they observe the Kumbh Mela at these four locations to commemorate this legend of the Amrita-Kumbh and take a bath in the adjoining rivers. In Nasik, it is held on the banks of the river Godavari, river Ganga in Haridwar, river Shipra in Ujjain and the confluence of the three rivers Ganga, Yamuna and Saraswati at Allahabad or Prayag (ancient name) in India.

The Purna Kumbh or Maha Kumbh, the biggest and the most auspicious fair, is held once every 12 years in one particular place and every fourth year on all the four places by rotation. Around 60 million people is said to attend the

Scene of Har Ki Paudi during Kumbh Mela

A hathyogi (practitioner of austere yoga) meditating on a single leg

Maha Kumbh Mela, making it the largest gathering anywhere in the world.

The pious Hindus believe that simply taking a bath in the holy waters of these places frees them and their ancestors back to the eighty-eighth generation from their past sins (karma). They hold that taking bath makes them and their ancestors eligible for liberation from the cycle of birth and death and ensures their salvation. Of course a pure lifestyle is also to be maintained after taking bath, otherwise nothing comes of this ritual. The ritual of bathing is carried out in the open and ideally on the banks of a river or stream with complete submergence of the body under water. Afterwards, an oblation is made to the sun god. The new moon day is held to be the most auspicious day for the ritual bath at Kumbh.

Kumbh Mela in India is attended by pilgrims coming from all walks of life. Many of these people often travel long distances to come to these places, tolerating many physical discomforts such as sleeping in the open air in near freezing weather. They willingly bear these difficulties just to have the chance of taking a bath in the sacred river at Kumbh Mela. The fair, however, is incomplete without the presence of the ascetics and sadhus. The Nagas, Urdhwavahurs, Parivrajakas, Shirshasins and Kalpvasis are a common sight at Kumbh Mela. These holy men or sadhus initiate the ritual bath at Kumbh Mela. Many of the devout Hindus assembled at Kumbh touch their feet and listen to them in the hope of gaining spiritual knowledge. This is followed by the collective dip in the holy waters.

Planetary positions during Kumbh

CITY	Jupiter	Sun	Moon
Haridwar	Aquarius	Aries	Sagittarius
Prayag (Allahabad)	Taurus	Capricorn	Capricorn
Nasik	Leo	Cancer	Cancer
Ujjain	Leo	Aries	Aries

Devotees taking holy dip in the Ganges during an Ardh Kumbh

MAHA KUMBH MELA

The Kumbh Mela is not a single event that is organised at regular intervals. While the Kumbh Mela is normally held after every four years, the Purna Kumbh Mela falls after every 12 years and is of greater importance than the Kumbh Mela. As per ancient Hindu mythology, some planets that are believed to affect the destiny of the human race align every 12 years and the Purna Kumbh Mela is held exactly during the time of this powerful planetary alignment.

The site for every Purna Kumbh is decided by the ascetics who jointly study the planetary positions and agree upon the location of observance. The Ardh Kumbha Mela(Half Kumbha Mela) is held after every six years or halfway between two Purna kumbh Melas; hence the name.

But the most important Kumbh Mela is the Maha Kumbh Mela(Great Kumbh Mela), that periodically falls every 144 years or after 12 Purna Kumbh Melas, and is held at Allahabad. A rarest of rare occasion, the Maha Kumbh Mela is looked upon by most Hindus as a once in a lifetime occasion that one can attend only with great fortune.

The Maha Kumbh Mela (Great Kumbh Mela) is organised at Prayag which is located near Allahabad in Uttar Pradesh. During this time, millions of devotees converge here to take a ceremonial dip in the Triveni Sangam - the confluence of the three great rivers Ganga, Jamuna and Saraswati meet. It is accepted to be the spot where four drops of the sacred nectar had fallen during the battle between the Devas (demigods) and Asuras(demons) over the Amrit-Kumbh(pot of nectar). The place is attended by millions of people who perform rituals here and also take a

People thronging river Godavari at Nasik on a Maha Kumbh

A physically challenged sadhu on the way to Har Ki Paudi at Haridwar

a ritual bath. The bathing is done in the open with complete submersion of the body under water and performing an oblation to the sun.

Religious Hindus attach great importance to this bathing ceremony and it forms the most important ritual of the Maha Kumbh Mela as also of the other Kumbh Melas. According to a popular legend, Lord Brahma (the God of Creation in Hindu Mythology) once proclaimed that taking a dip in the holy River Ganga can liberate mankind from its sins. The Hindus believe that bathing in the sacred waters at the Kumbh Mela will purge them and their ancestors back to the eighty-eighth generation off all evil and sin. This would make them suitable to attain moksha (salvation) from the cycle of life, death and rebirth.

The inner significance of this ritual bath lies in understanding the true implication of the Samudra-Manthan episode. The "amrit" or nectar implies the divine knowledge and strength that lies within each of us. The churning of the ocean symbolizes that each of us must judiciously churn our own inner self to gain this knowledge.

The other important activities associated to the Maha Kumbh Mela include singing of bhajans (devotional songs), discussions on religious matters, mass feeding of holy men and women and the poor, and gatherings where religious doctrines are debated and determined.

The first Maha Kumbh of the 21st century and also of this millennium was held in 2001 at Prayag . The grand religious congregation was attended by around 60 million people, consisting of men, women and children, thousands of sadhus (monks) and also more than 65,000 foreigners from abroad curious to get a glimpse of this grand affair.

Foreigners with a sadhu during a Kumbh at Haridwar

ARDHA KUMBH MELA

A mass pilgrimage for the Hindu community of India, the Kumbh Mela or Kumbh fair is rumoured to be one of the largest congregation of sages, yogis, ascetics, mendicants, men, women and children on the planet. Around 90 million people from around the world are expected to attend the Purna Kumbh Mela in Haridwar during January-April, 2010, making it the largest gathering anywhere in the world.

Every sixth year after a Purna Kumbh Mela sees an Ardh Kumbh Mela taking place. In the Hindi language the word "Ardh" stands for "half" and "Mela" means "fair". The "Ardh Kumbh Mela" is called so because it is held at the sixth year and marks the halfway stage between the celebration of the Purna Kumbh Melas every 12 years. The Ardh Mela (half Fair) takes place six years after the Maha Kumbh in each of the four aforementioned locations by turns.

During the period of the Kumbh Mela, a tent city comes up for over a month by the banks of the river (of the spot where the fair is held) to provide shelter to thousands of pilgrims. A number of Hindu religious organisations set up camps in the fair grounds during this period. Of late many Indian and multi-national companies provide make-shift tents with all the modern gadgets fitted in them at the Kumbh sites. One of such multi-national companies is Cocks & Kings of Switzerland. In different spots of the region, folk theatre groups get busy enacting different stories and scenes from sacred Hindu texts.

The myth of the "Amrita-Kumbha" is performed as a dramatic performance which is lapped up by the

Devotees taking holy dips in Sangam at Prayag on Makar Sankranti

assembled devotees. People from all classes of society come in multitudes to the fair grounds driven by the desire to take a dip in the sacred river waters as well as to receive the blessings of the great holy men assembled in the fair. Many of the devotees live in camps and ashrams (temples) for the whole duration of the mela and lead a sacred life. Such a living is called "Kalpavas" and those who live thus are called "Kalpvasi".

Like its bigger counterparts (Purna Kumbh Mela, Maha Kumbha Mela) and smaller counterparts (Magh Mela) the purpose of organising Ardh Kumbh Mela is to commemorate the legend of the struggle between the gods and demons over the Amrita Kumbha (pot of nectar) and draws innumerable crowds who believe in the Hindu Puranas and come in quest of purifying their soul before entering the realm of god.

A seasoned Naga with long locks of hair in a crowd of devotees at Prayag

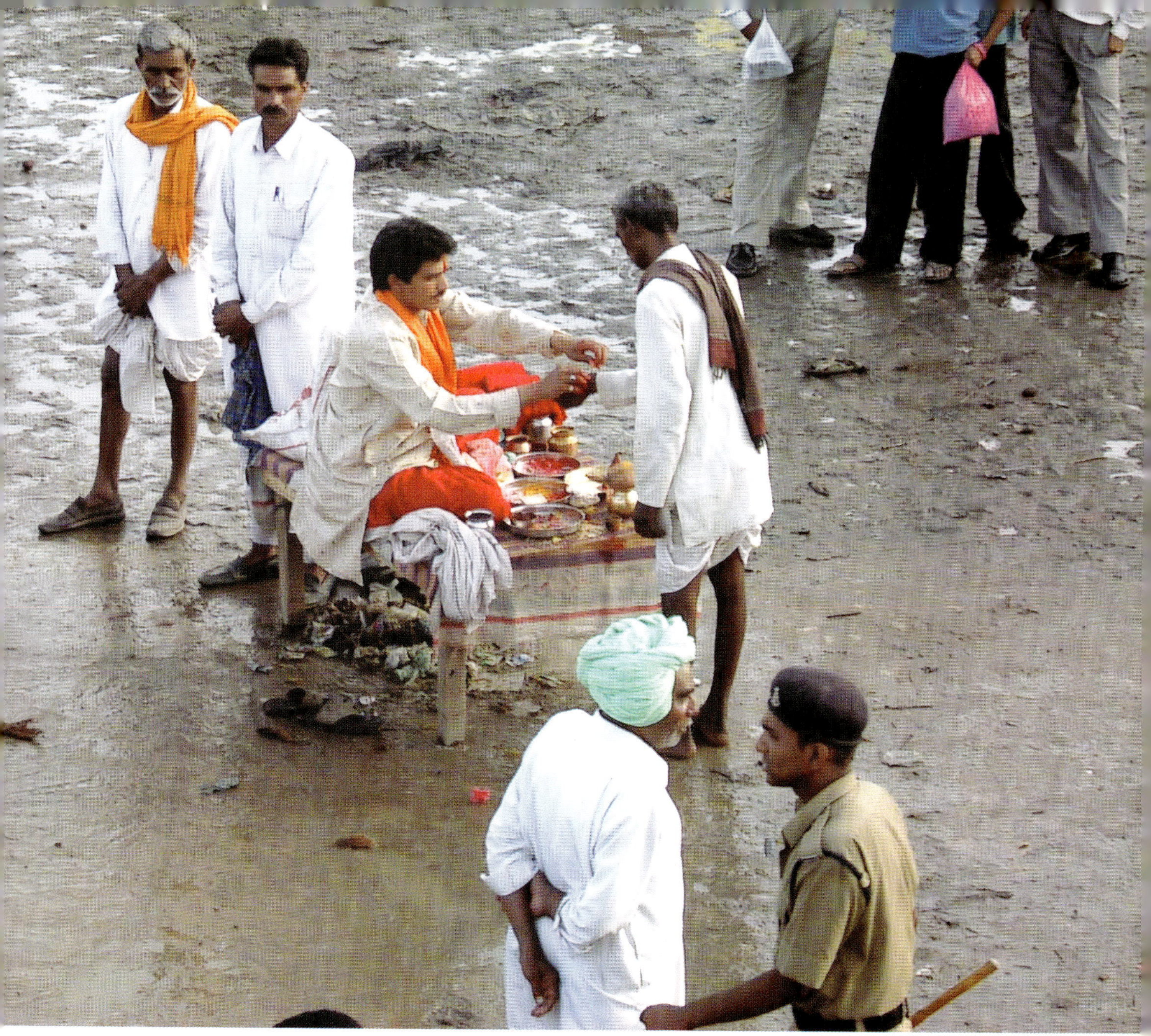

A Sadhu performing rites to ward off evils of solar eclipse

A kalpavasi peforming religious rites in the month of Magh

MAGH MELA

The Magh Mela is one of the greatest annual religious affairs for Hindus. Hindu mythology considers the origin of the Magh Mela to be the beginning of the Universe. An important occasion, the Magh Mela is held every year on the banks of Triveni Sangam in Prayag near Allahabad in Uttar Pradesh.

In accordance with the traditional Hindu calendar followed in North India, this holy fair is organised every year during the Hindu month of Magh (corresponding to mid January - mid February of the Gregorian calendar); hence the name. The Magh Mela is, however, not confined only to the month of Magh and the important bathing dates are spread over a period of 45 days. The Magh Mela is actually a smaller version of Kumbh Mela. Hence it is also known as mini Kumbh Mela.

Every year, the Magh Mela commences on the day of Makkar Sankranti in January, which is the first important bathing day according to the religious Hindu calendar. It begins with multitudes of pilgrims taking a holy dip at the Sangam on auspicious dates. A large number of people arrive here annually and stay in makeshift houses or tents at the Sangam, spending the entire month of Magh in prayers. This period is known as "Kalpvas". Those who religiously observe the "Kalpvas" are known as "Kalpvasis".

The ancient Hindu Vedas mention a "Kalp" to be the period equal to the total number of years in the four yugas - Satyug, Treta, Dwapar and Kalyug. This adds up to several millions of years. It is said that by piously observing a "Kalpavas", a devotee overcomes the sins in his/her previous birth and escapes the cycle of Janma(birth) and Karma (actions). During each day of the Magh Mela, a Kalpvasi has to take a dip at the Ganges on sunrise praying to the rising sun. Majority of the Kalpvasis partake only a meal a day. After observing 12 Kalpavas, a Kalpavasi has to donate his/her bed and all his belongings (a ritual known as "Shayya Daan").

The Uttar Pradesh government annually makes special arrangements for the devotees during this time. A greater number of buses ply to let the pilgrims have their journey in peace and without any inconvenience. A township of tents specially comes up on the banks of the Sangam to provide shelter to the visiting millions who turn up from all over the country. Adequate medical and security arrangements are made to avoid any untoward incidents. "Lost and Found" camps are also set up and manned by the local police to prevent anyone getting missing during the days of the fair.

Every twelfth year, the Magh Mela is transformed into the Kumbha Mela. Uttar Pradesh is flooded with millions of pilgrims who arrive here during this time to attend this grand event.

In 2010, Magh Mela commences on January 11 and ends on February 23.

Elephant-riding sadhus going to Kumbh Mela

Nagas jumping into holy Ganges during a Kumbh Mela

RITUALS

Kumbh Mela is one of the most auspicious Hindu pilgrimages. Millions of devotees, sadhu, tourists, men, women and kids gather in huge crowds to participate in this holy and auspicious pilgrimage that is celebrated from the dawn to dusk. Major activities or rituals followed during the event are:

- Holy Bath : Even if many people don't know some of the detailed rituals of this pilgrimage, the most famous, credited, trusted, enjoyed and respected rituals is to take bath in holy rivers. Holy dip in the river for on the day of Mela (the time of very auspicious composition of the stars and constellations) is considered to be a purifying act among Hindus.
- Religious Discussions : Many religious gurus, sadhus, astrologers and holy men gather on this day to discuss and distribute the knowledge of scriptures, Vedas, Upanishads and other holy texts.
- Devotional Singing : On the occasion of Kumbh Mela devotees surrender themselves to the serenity of God by singing devotional songs and bhajans in different languages. With millions of devotees gathered together and becomes an extremely divine atmosphere.
- Mass Feeding : Charity in form of money, food, clothes is considered very sacred in Hindu tradition and customs. The Kumbha Mela is a perfect platform for these activities as many holy men, poor men & women, disabled people also gather here.
- Religious assemblies : Many religious leaders organise these assemblies during the Mela to discuss and standardise the doctrines.

Nagas performing tantric rites

Scene of a mass feeding at Nasik during Kumbh Mela

Mahanths (high priests of various religious seats) taking part in a religious discourse

A musical soiree in Kumbh Mela

A shirshasinse meditating standing on his head

ACTIVITIES

- On the day of new moon, the first set of rituals start at 3.00 am, when the first set of pilgrims gather to take bath in the holy river. There is custom to shave heads before taking bath in the river and people are seen chanting "Jai Ganga Maiya" while taking bath.
- At the time of dawn with the first ray of sun, Nagas sect of sadhus are seen leading processions followed by different other sect of sadhus in groups .These groups of Sadhus move towards the "Sangam" in great grandeur, so that each of these sect try and overpower the magnitude of grandeur of other groups. These chorus forms a magical environment in the atmosphere.
- After these acts of purifying themselves, by taking bath, pilgrims wear fresh clothes and proceed to different areas of the fair to discuss, listen, and participate in ongoing religious activities.

Energizing the mind and soul

The atmosphere of the Kumbh Mela comprising of holy activities and purifying acts provides the perfect atmosphere to wash away one's sins and achieve salvation, which is to become one to God Almighty.

At this phase a man detaches himself to worldly materialistic pleasures and becomes one with god to realize the purity of his soul.

Picture of Natraj (dancing Shiva)

SIGNIFICANCE OF KUMBH

A hathyogi (practitioner of austere yoga) showing his body flexibility

Religious Significance :

For any common man attending the Kumbh Mela it is a once in a lifetime opportunity. According to the Hindu mythology, this Mela is supposed to be the "king of Tirths", as all holy men, rishi-muni, religious scholars, astute devotees, gather here to attain salvation by taking holy bath in rivers having religious significance. It is believed that bathing during Kumbh cures the bather of all sins and evils and grants the bather, salvation.

Commercial Significance :

The traders, shopkeepers and many craftsmen observe this occasion as an opportunity for better and exponential profits. Apart from all the holy men there are also the common masses, kids and ladies for whom this sacred trip is also a means of holidaying in the best manner.

Health Significance :

It is also believed that particular celestial positions at the time of Kumbh Yog, water of river Ganga is charged positively by enhanced electromagnetic radiations of the Sun, Moon and the Jupiter, the flux of which also varies in accordance with positions and the phases of the moon, and also by the + and - signs of the sun spots. Thus, water of Ganga is charged with positive healing effects and a dip in this water is considered beneficial from health point of view.

A sharshinse meditating standing on his head

Sadhus smoking ganja pipe

Naga sadhus

Devotees gathered at a Kumbh Mela

A tantric medidating at Asthi Prawah Ghat in Haridwar

GHATS

Kumbh Mela is the largest congregation of pilgrims at a single place in the history of human civilization. Large numbers of people travel from far long places to Haridwar for participating in this mega religious fair.

Ardh kumbh Mela is considered the main holy festival of Hindus and devotees wait for the festival very eagerly as the fair is conducted after every 6 years.

People believe that taking holy bath in the sacred Ganga at the time of Kumbh Mela is very auspicious and is the mean to attain salvation.

One can be released from the cycle of life and get in close proximity to the Almighty by taking holy dip during the Ardh Kumbh fair. The holy rivers at the site of Ardh kumbh Mela offers purity, wealth, fertility and wash away the sins of those who bath in it.

There are many bathing ghats at the holy city of Haridwar, the main ghat is Har Ki Pauri and other important ones are Asthi Parwah Ghat, Subhash Ghat and Gau Ghat.

- **Asthi Parwah Ghat**

  The Asthi Parwah Ghat is the ghat meant for immersing ashes of the departed souls of the family. It is believed that the cooling waters of the river will bestow salvation upon the departed soul. The ghat is located in south of the main Ganga temple.

❖ Subhash Ghat

Subhash Ghat is the ghat adjacent to the Har-Ki-Pauri with a statue of the freedom fighter Netaji Subhash Chandra Bose. A dispensary to provide medical help to the visitors and help them is available on this ghat. The dispensary is run by the Sewa Samiti, a voluntary organization.

❖ Gau Ghat

Gau ghat is present in south of Subhash Ghat. The word "gau" means cow, so this is the ghat where people seek atonement for the sin of cow slaughter. Death ceremonies are completed with the pious act of donating a cow. The sin of killing a cow is "equal to the sin of killing a Brahmin".

A naked Naga Sadhu praying in the Ganges

A sadhu with holy ash smeared on his body

THE SADHUS AT THE KUMBH MELA

The sadhus and other holy men are an integral part of the Kumbh Mela. Pilgrims who attend the Kumbh Mela come to see and listen to these men, in order to gain spiritual enlightenment.

There are various types of sadhus:

- Nagas - naked sadhus who smear their bodies with ash and have long matted hair. Constant exposure to the weather makes them resistant to temperature extremes. Their eyes are bloodshot from constantly smoking charas (marijuana), which they believe aids enlightenment.
- Urdhwavahurs - who have emaciated bodies from rigid spiritual practices.
- Parivajakas - who have taken a vow of silence.
- Shirshasinse - who remain standing, sleep with their heads resting on a vertical pole, and meditate standing on their heads.
- Kalpvasis - who remain by the river banks and devote their time to meditating, performing rituals, and bathing numerous times a day.

A sadhu showing stunts at Haridwar

Nagas proceeding to take holy dip in the Ganges

A boy posing as Lord Shiva on the Occasion of Kumbh Mela

Nagas taking out a procession during Kumbh Mela

THE GLORY OF HARIDWAR

Haridwar, the holy city lies at the foot of the Shivalik range of the Himalayas. Legend goes that when Lord Shiva sent Ganga to quench the thirst of the people, she extricated herself from the matted locks of Lord Shiva and descended to the plains at Haridwar. From here, the Ganga proceeds eastwards and southwards through Allahabad, Varanasi, Patna, Calcutta towards Ganga Sagar, where it meets the sea.

The holy city of Haridwar is home to some of the most sacred Hindu rituals. Round the year, devotees from all over the country flock here in their thousands to perform "poojas" or prayers. Haridwar is known for the Kumbh and Ardh Kumbh fairs that are held marking the 12 years of solar cycle. Millions of devotees and visitors take a dip in the holiest of Hindu rivers at this time, to attain salvation. Another attraction is the enchanting "Aarti" at "Har Ki Pauri" which captives the beholder with hundreds of burning wick lamps floating down the Ganga.

It is said that you can attain salvation by praying to Lord Vishnu (Hari) or Lord Shiva and hence this sacred spot is known both as Haridwar and Hardwar.

Haridwar is one of the seven holiest places according to Hindu mythology, as the Gods are believed to have left their footprints in Haridwar. Due to its geographical location too, Haridwar stands as the gateway to the other three important pilgrimages of Uttrakhand namely, Rishikesh, Badrinath and Kedarnath. Referred to as Mayapuri, Gangadwar, and Mokshadwar in the ancient scriptures and epics, Haridwar has always remained a major pilgrimage for the Hindus.

Picture of a hill-top near Har Ki Paudi from which entire Haridwar can be viewed

A GLIMPSE OF HARIDWAR

Haridwar is the venue of the Maha Kumbh of 2010. Here is detailed information about various religious places, rituals and fairs and festivals of Haridwar.

Har Ki Pauri

This sacred Ghat was constructed by King Vikramaditya in memory of his brother Bhartrihari. It is believed that Bhartrihari eventually came to Haridwar to meditate by the banks of holy Ganga. When he died, his brother constructed a Ghat in his name which later came to be known as Hari-Ki-Pauri. This sacred bathing ghat is also known as Brahmakund. The reflection of golden hues of floral diyas in the river Ganga is the most enchanting sight in the twilight during the Ganga Arti ceremony .

Maya Devi Temple

This is an ancient temple of Maya Devi, the Adhisthatri deity of Haridwar, known as one of the Siddhpeethas. Said to be the place where the heart and navel of goddess Sati had fallen.

Har Ki Pauri

Maya Devi Temple

Daksha Mahadev Temple

Daksha Mahadev Temple

The ancient temple of Daksha Mahadev is situated in the south Kankhal town .The mythological story about this place is that King Daksha Prajapati, father of Sati (Lord Shiva's first wife) performed yagya at this place. Daksha Prajapati did not invite Lord Shiva and Sati felt insulted . Therefore, she burnt herself in the yagya Kund. This incident provoked the disciples and followers of Mahadev who killed King Daksha, but later on Lord Mahadev brought him back to life. Daksha Mahadev temple is thus a tribute to this legend .

Chandi Devi Temple

The temple of Chandi Devi is atop the Neel Parvat on the other bank of river Ganga. It is 3 kms trek from Chandighat. Legend has it that the army chief Chanda-Munda of a local demon King Shumbh- Nishumbha was killed by goddess Chandi here after which the place got the name Chandi Devi . It is believed that the main statue was established by the Adi Shankracharya in 8th century A.D. One can reach here by trolley through ropeway or on foot.

Mansa Devi Temple

The temple of Goddess Mansa Devi is situated at the top of Bilwa Parwat. Here one statue of the Goddess has three mouths and five arms while the other statue has eight arms. The beautiful view of the city can be seen from this place. The temple can be reached by trolley through ropeway or on foot.

Chandi Devi Temple

Mansa Devi Temple

Kali Mata Mandir

Kali Mata Mandir

In memory of his beloved father late Amar Nath Guptaji, Shri Sunil Gupta inspired and visualized this sacred Kali Mata temple at a holy place like Haridwar. Kali Mata Mandir has been designed as per norms of Indian Temple Architecture and Hindu Vastu Shastra.

Bhimgoda Tank

This tank is at a distance of about 1 km from Har ki Pauri. It is said that while Pandavas were going to Himalayas through Haridwar, Bhim made this tank with the blow of his knee.

Parad Shivling

It is situated in Harihar Ashram at Kankhal. Shivling weighing about 150 kg and Rudraksha tree are main attractions here.

Other Places of Interest

Haridwar has several other beautifully made Ashrams/temples of significance such as ShantiKunj, Jairam Ashram, Bhuma Niketan, Bharat Mata Mandir, Vaishnav Devi Temple, Radha Krishan temple, Shravan Nath Math, Pawan Dham, Bilkeshwar Mahadev Temple, Neeleshwar temple, Doodhadari temple, Shahi Gurudwara, Parmarth Ashram, Prem Nagar Ashram,Ma Anand Mai Ashram etc. All of these places are worth seeing.

Lord Shiva

Parad Shivling

A temple at Nasik

Gathering of devotee during a Kumbh Mela at Prayag

A view of temples in Nasik during a Maha Kumbh Mela

A sadhu dressing as Lord Shiva in a Kumbh Mela

A priest sitting on a throne in middle of the Ganges at Prayag

FAIR & FESTIVALS

Haridwar is one place where fairs are being organised with full enthusiasm round the year, such as Somwati Amavasya, Kartik Poornima, Shravan Poornima, Ganga Dussehra and other important bathing dates of Hindu calendar. The Kanwad Mela during the month of Shravana is very popular among masses in which lacs of devotees of Lord Shiva come to Haridwar to take holy water of river Ganga.

Apart from these, Kumbh mela and Ardh Kumbh mela at the interval of 12 and 6 years respectively do not need any more introduction. District administration also organise 'Haridwar Mahotsava', a 3-4 day cultural festival on the bank of river Ganga and 'Ayurveda Mahotsava'. Besides this 'Urs' is organized annually at the holy dargah of Piran Kaliyar in which people of all sects participate and pray for their well being.

Scene of aarti at Har Ki Paudi in Haridwar at dusk

TRAVEL TO HARIDWAR

Haridwar, the holy city of India is accessible through air, rail and road.

How to reach Haridwar by Air : The nearest airport is the Jolly Grant in Dehradun. However, it is convenient to use roads or rail to Delhi and then take the flight to Haridwar.

How to reach Haridwar by Rail : The major pilgrimage center of Haridwar is well connected by trains to almost all the major cities in India.

How to reach Haridwar by Road : Haridwar is well connected to the major cities in India. The National Highway No.45 crosses the city of Haridwar and links it with Delhi, which assures a comfortable travel to Haridwar.

Foreigners enjoying the mirth of Kumbh Mela

Scene of river Shipra at Ujjain during a Maha Kumbh Mela

Mahanths (high priests of religious seats) riding an elephant to Prayag

A snake charmer

Sadhus intoxicated after consuming cannabis and marijuana and puffing ganja pipe

A sadhu showing his magical power riding on a horse

A boy waiting to perform the last rites of his father

Devotees at Ujjain after taking Shahi Snan (royal bath)

A sadhu with his retinue going to Ardh Kumbh in Haridwar

A view of an akhara (a wrestling arena and place of religious debates) in Varanasi during a Maha Kumbh in Prayag

A sadhu offering water to a deity

A sadhu whiffing a ganja pipe

TRAVEL ADIVSORY

The 2010 Kumbh Mela is taking place in Haridwar at the foothills of the Himalayas in Uttarakhand. Here are some travel tips to keep in mind when planning your trip.

- Roads will be extremely congested and traffic diverted well before Haridwar. Therefore, taking the train is the most convenient option of getting there. Be sure to make a reservation well in advance. Find out about options for train travel and booking a ticket. (Indian Railways reservations are open 90 days in advance of travel date).
- Do take into account the weather when attending the Kumbh Mela, especially if you want to bathe in the river. Haridwar is quite cold during the winter, but starts warming up in February. By April, the weather will be hot there.
- The massive crowds of millions of people on the important bathing days can be dangerous (people have been killed in stampedes), so do take extra care on these days.
- Reserve a hotel with a view of the Ganges River and Har Ki Pauri ghat. If you don't mind splurging, Haveli Hari Ganga is a recommended option. Double rooms cost around $150 per night. The hotel also provides luxury tented accommodations for the Mela.
- Government tent accommodations are also available. However, they cater more to the masses of Indian tourists.

- There is a hill above Har Ki Pauri ghat, where you can safely view the goings on away from the crowds.
- Dress is loose, comfortable clothes in dark or earth colors.
- Giving money is considered to be an important aspect of pilgrimage to the Kumbh Mela. Place money at the feet of sadhus if seeking an audience with them. An amount ending with one rupee is considered to be most auspicious (eg. 51 rupees, 101 rupees).
- Not all "holy" people who attend the Kumbh Mela are authentic. Do be careful of con artists.
- If you would like the added security of visiting the Kumbh Mela with a tour group, there are quite a few companies that conduct escorted tours to the Kumbh Mela. These include Divine Travels, Kumbhmela.net, and Royal Indian Voyages. This type of travel can often provide access to experiences that it would be difficult to have on your own, including access to renowned spiritual leaders.

A Naga showing martial art

Scene of a Magh Mela in Haridwar

Naked sadhus (Nagas) making a beeline at a Goḍavadi ghat in Nasik

Religious gurus sailing in a chariot-like boat to Prayag

Hawkers selling garlands of rudraksha and crystal at Har Ki Paudi

A sadhu engaged in antyesti (last rites)

Rows of Nagas and other devotees in Ujjain ready to take dip in Shipra river at Ujjain

Mendicants in Haridwar hopeful of getting alms